W9-BNQ-248

MONTGOMERY-FLOYD REGIONAL LIBRARY
BLACKSBURG BRANCH

A TASTE OF
SPAIN

Bob Goodwin and Candi Perez

Thomson Learning
New York

C. 1

Titles in this series

A TASTE OF

Britain	Italy
The Caribbean	Japan
China	Mexico
France	Spain
India	West Africa

Cover *Olive groves in Andalusia.*

Title page *The Alcazar, or palace, in Segovia, built during the Middle Ages.*

First published in the
United States in 1995 by
Thomson Learning
115 Fifth Avenue
New York, NY 10003

First published in Great Britain in 1994 by
Wayland (Publishers) Ltd.

U.K. version copyright © 1994 Wayland (Publishers) Ltd.

U.S. version copyright © 1995 Thomson Learning

Library of Congress Cataloging-in-Publication Data
Goodwin, Bob
A taste of Spain / Bob Goodwin and Candi Perez.
p.   cm.—(Food around the world)
Includes bibliographical references and index.
ISBN 1-56847-188-2
1. Cookery, Spanish—Juvenile literature.
2. Food habits—Spain—Juvenile literature.
3. Spain—Social life and customs—Juvenile literature.
[1. Cookery, Spanish. 2. Food habits—Spain. 3. Spain—
Social life and customs.] I. Perez, Candi. II. Title. III. Series.
TX723.5.S7G66   1995
394.1'2'0946—dc20   94-30606

Printed in Italy

Contents

Spain and its people

The land

Spain is the second largest country in western Europe and occupies an area of land known as the Iberian Peninsula. The northern coast faces the Atlantic Ocean and the Bay of Biscay. The Pyrenees mountain range runs along the northern border between Spain and France. To the east and south is the Mediterranean Sea. At the southern tip of Spain is the British military base of Gibraltar, which overlooks the narrow

A mountain village in southern Spain. Gibraltar and North Africa are on the horizon.

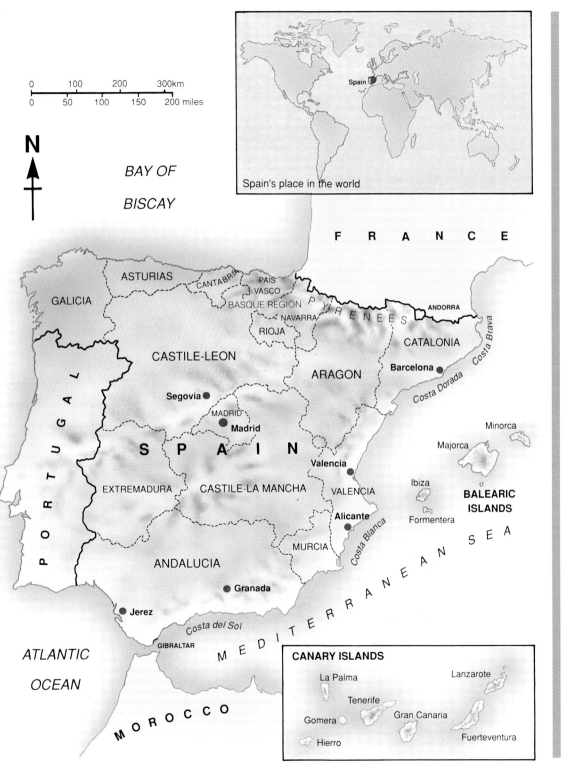

Spain's place in the world

0 100 200 300km
0 50 100 150 200 miles

N

BAY OF

BISCAY

FRANCE

ASTURIAS

CANTABRIA

PAIS
VASCO

BASQUE REGION

GALICIA

NAVARRA

PYRENEES

ANDORRA

RIOJA

CASTILE-LEON

CATALONIA

Costa Brava

ARAGON

Barcelona

Costa Dorada

Segovia

MADRID

Madrid

S P A I N

P O R T U G A L

Minorca

Majorca

Valencia

EXTREMADURA

CASTILE-LA MANCHA

VALENCIA

Ibiza

BALEARIC
ISLANDS

Alicante

Formentera

Costa Blanca

MURCIA

M E D I T E R R A N E A N   S E A

ANDALUCIA

Granada

Jerez

Costa del Sol

GIBRALTAR

ATLANTIC

OCEAN

M O R O C C O

CANARY ISLANDS

La Palma

Lanzarote

Tenerife

Gomera

Gran Canaria

Hierro

Fuerteventura

A taste of Spain

A country scene from central Spain. Notice the ancient castle in the background.

Strait of Gibraltar between the Mediterranean Sea and the Atlantic Ocean. To the west of the country is Portugal. The Balearic Islands in the Mediterranean and the Canary Islands, 750 miles southwest in the Atlantic off the coast of Africa, also belong to Spain.

Mainland Spain is divided into seventeen regions, with different customs and traditions. The things that people usually think of as typically Spanish come from the region of Andalusia (in Spanish, Andalucía) in the far south. This is the home of guitars and flamenco dancing. The popular tourist area Costa del Sol is in Andalusia as well.

The people

Spain has a population of about
40 million people. In the past, most
Spaniards made a living working on
small farms. However, in the last fifteen
years, more and more people have left
the countryside to work in the towns
and cities, and some of the old villages
are like ghost towns.

The Spanish are famous for their flamenco dancing. This exciting and complicated dance is usually accompanied by guitar music, while the audience claps out the rhythm.

The languages of Spain

Almost all Spaniards speak Castilian,
which is usually referred to as Spanish.
But three other languages are also
spoken in Spain.

In Galicia in the northwest, the people
speak Galician, which is similar to

Above *A small village in the Basque country.*

Below *A harbor inlet in Minorca, one of the Balearic Islands.*

Portuguese. The Galicians are descended from the Celts, an ancient people from western Europe.

At the western end of the Pyrenees is the Basque country where the Basque language is spoken. Basque is completely different from all other languages and is very complicated. Some people think that the Basques were the first people to live in Europe, thousands of years ago.

At the eastern end of the Pyrenees is Catalonia where the people speak Catalan, which is like a mixture of Spanish, French, and Italian. In Valencia and the Balearic Islands, most people speak a dialect of Catalan.

History

The aqueduct at Segovia is one of more than two hundred aqueducts built by the Romans when Spain was part of the Roman Empire. These stone waterways brought fresh water from springs that were often many miles away.

Throughout its history, Spain has been invaded and conquered many times. The first people to conquer all of Spain were the Romans, whose conquest began in 218 B.C. It took two hundred years to conquer the entire country. The Romans built long, straight roads and an irrigation system to bring water to dry areas of the country. Some Roman aqueducts still stand today, such as the one at Segovia.

The Romans ruled Spain for five hundred years, until they were defeated

Above *The Alhambra is a magnificent palace built for the Muslim rulers in the thirteenth century.*

Below *This statue in Granada shows Columbus reporting his discoveries to Queen Isabella.*

by the Visigoths, who ruled for the next three hundred years. During this time, Spain became a Christian country. In A.D. 711, Muslims from North Africa invaded and conquered most of the country. By this time, Spain was faced with food and water shortages. The Muslims rebuilt the aqueducts and improved the irrigation systems. They introduced a type of wheat which was easy to grow and made famine less likely. They also introduced many new foods such as eggplants, carrots, and oranges. Many Spanish dishes are made with these ingredients, often using recipes similar to the ones used by the Muslims.

Although most people accepted Muslim rule, groups of Christians continued to fight against the Muslims throughout the next eight hundred years. In 1492, they recaptured Spain from the Muslims. That same year Christopher Columbus, supported by the king and queen of Spain, set out on his voyage across the Atlantic Ocean and arrived at what is now known as the Americas.

The sixteenth century is considered the Golden Age of Spain. During that time, Spain was the most powerful and important country in Europe. It had established a vast empire that included most of South America and parts of North America.

Spanish explorers in the New World brought back many foods, such as corn, tomatoes, and potatoes, that were new to Europeans.

By the beginning of the nineteenth century, Spain was less powerful, and the Spanish Empire began to fall apart. Between 1936 and 1939 there was a civil war in Spain. General Francisco Franco and his followers won the war and Franco ruled the country as a dictator. In 1975, when Franco died, Prince Juan Carlos was crowned king of Spain. He is very popular with Spaniards because he decided that Spain should have a democratic government. The first free elections were held in 1977.

Today, Spain is an important member of the European Community, which it joined in 1986. It was host to soccer's 1982 World Cup, the 1992 Olympic Games, and the World Trade Fair (Expo '92). In 1992, Madrid, the capital city, was named European City of Culture.

Madrid, with a population of over 3.5 million, is an exciting and beautiful city in the heart of Spain.

Food production

Farming

Farming in Spain varies greatly because of the differences in climate throughout the country. The north is wet, and the south is very dry. Much of the center of Spain is a high, flat plain known as the Meseta, which is cold in winter and extremely hot in the summer. The Meseta is also dry. The main crops are wheat and corn. Farmers here raise sheep and goats. Hundreds of years ago, farmers of the Meseta gathered enormous flocks of sheep, which they herded around Spain like cattle in a Hollywood Western. Although the huge flocks are gone, there are still plenty of sheep on the Meseta.

A shepherd of the Meseta, the high, flat plain in central Spain, with his flock of sheep.

In the wetter northern regions, farmers grow fruits such as apples, pears, plums, peaches, melons, and figs. In the southern areas, pomegranates, avocados, and citrus fruits are grown. Marmalade, a kind of bitter orange jam, is made with oranges from Seville, the capital of Andalusia. Valencia is another area

An orange plantation near Seville.

A taste of Spain

Planting rice in Valencia, where there is plenty of water to irrigate the rice fields.

Blossoming almond trees.

where oranges are grown. Rice is also grown in Valencia because there is plenty of water for irrigation.

Spain is generally too hot to produce many dairy products. However, in the northwest the climate is cooler than in the rest of the country and heavy rainfalls produce lush pastures. There are some dairy farms.

The mild climate in the Canary Islands is ideal for farming, but the land is hilly. To solve the problem, farmers have built stone terraces filled with

earth brought in from elsewhere. The main crops are bananas and tomatoes, many of which are exported.

Almonds are grown in the south and in the Balearic Islands. Almond trees are a beautiful sight in the springtime when they blossom.

Spain is one of the world's largest producers of olives and olive oil. Olives are grown all over the country. In parts of Extremadura and Andalusia, the olive groves stretch as far as the eye can see. The trees are neatly arranged so that

Steep terraced fields on the Canary Islands.

Above left *Olive groves in Andalusia stretch as far as the eye can see.*

Above right *A typical countryside scene with huge olive trees and wildflowers.*

trucks and harvesting machines can be used. Even in Roman times, olives and olive oil were exported to England. Recently, archaeologists found some two-thousand-year-old Spanish olives at the bottom of the Thames River.

The owners of most small farms have a few olive trees and almond trees, but they make very little money from the sale of these crops. They generally keep them to eat themselves.

Wine

The Spanish have been growing grapes and making wine for thousands of years. Many farmers harvest a few grapes each year to make their own wine. Often a group of farmers in a particular village will collect all their produce together. These groups are called cooperatives. By working together, farmers can share the cost of expensive machinery to make their farms more efficient.

Picking grapes in Valencia. The grapes will be used to make wine.

Above *This man is sampling some hundred-year-old sherry.*

Below *A vineyard in the region of Rioja.*

In some areas, wine is big business. Sherry, the most famous Spanish wine, comes from the area around Jerez. The English had difficulty pronouncing Jerez correctly, so they called it "sherry." Sherry became such a popular drink among the English that some English people moved to Spain to produce it. Today, many of the Spanish families that make sherry have English ancestors and English surnames.

Wine from the region of Rioja is reknowned in Spain and is now also becoming popular throughout Europe.

Fishing

For many years, people from villages on the coasts of southern and eastern Spain were very poor. They made a living by catching fish. In the last thirty years, although some fishing continues, fishing villages such as Fuengirola and Benidorm have become popular tourist resorts. On the Atlantic coast of the northwest, fishing is an important industry. Refrigerated trains carry the fish overnight to the big cities, so there is always fresh fish available in Madrid early in the morning.

Above *Benidorm, on the Costa Blanca, was once a small fishing village but has now become a busy tourist resort full of huge skyscrapers.*

Left *An old fishing village on the Costa Blanca.*

Cooking ingredients

Above *Some nearly ripe olives.*

Olive oil is one of the most important ingredients in Spanish cookery. The oil is made by crushing and pressing the olives. Olives are also a popular cooking ingredient, and people eat them as *tapas*, or snacks. Olives that are to be eaten are usually picked green and then cured. Black olives are the ones that have been left on the tree to ripen. Olive oil is usually made from black olives.

Spanish onions are famous throughout the world. Many Spanish recipes begin with frying onions or garlic, or both, in

Right *Garlic for sale at an open-air market.*

olive oil. In southern Spain, people often like to have garlic, salt, and olive oil on their toast.

Chorizo is a highly seasoned cured sausage made from pork. It is eaten on its own or can be added to a stew. Ham is also used in stews and eaten as a *tapa*. Most *tapa* bars and households have a leg of ham hanging up in the kitchen. Spanish ham is specially cured, giving it a strong flavor and chewy texture.

Above *Chorizo, a popular Spanish sausage, hanging up in a butcher's shop.*

Left *An early morning delivery of freshly baked bread.*

Spanish bread has a cakelike texture that makes it very filling. Most families buy fresh bread from the bakery every day.

Sweet peppers, carrots, potatoes, and tomatoes are the favorite vegetables for making stews. Usually two or three different kinds of vegetables are cooked together in olive oil. In addition to vegetables, a stew may be made with meat, lentils, chickpeas, or beans.

Spanish cheese is usually quite hard and can have a very strong flavor. The most popular cheese is called Manchego because it comes from the region of La Mancha. It is made from sheep's milk. Cheese is not used much in Spanish cooking, but it is a popular *tapa*.

Saffron is made by collecting and drying the tiny orange stigmas inside the petals of a crocus. It has a strong bitter flavor and makes the food it is cooked with yellow. Saffron is used in stews and in a rice dish called paella.

This man is picking the flowers of a saffron crocus. The orange-red stigmas are removed from the flower and dried to produce saffron threads.

Mealtimes

Spaniards love to spend a long time eating large meals. Almost everyone drinks wine with their meals, including the children, who are given a little wine mixed with water.

Traditionally, *la comida* (lunch) is the most important meal of the day. It is

A Spanish family enjoying la comida.

eaten in the middle of the afternoon, at about two or three o'clock, and often the whole family, including young children and grandparents who live nearby, eat together. *La comida* usually includes vegetables, fish, meat, and dessert. After the meal most people have a *siesta*, or nap, for an hour or so. Some people do not have to go back to work after lunch, but there is school in the afternoons. Spanish children do not have a bedtime and often stay up as late as their parents. They seldom get tired or sleepy because they have had a *siesta* after their late lunch.

In the big cities, like Madrid and Barcelona, people usually work or go to school too far away to come home for *la comida*. For these families, *la cena* (supper), rather than lunch, becomes the main meal. In more traditional places, like Seville, *la cena* is a small meal. It may be just a sandwich; this is called a *bocadillo*, which means "mouthful." Many people do not bother with supper; instead, the whole family goes out to eat *tapas* (see page 26).

People having a snack at an open-air café in Madrid.

Churro, *a spiral doughnut, is a favorite treat for most Spaniards.*

For breakfast, adults may have a cup of coffee and some toast in a coffee bar on their way to work. Children may have some fruit juice and take a *bocadillo* to school to eat during break time. But almost everyone likes to have *churros* for breakfast once in a while. They are like deep-fried doughnuts in the shape of giant twisted pencils. One popular way to eat a *churro* is to dip it into a thick, sweet hot chocolate.

At about six o'clock in the evening is *merienda*, when people drink hot chocolate or coffee. *Merienda* is never complete without a rich cake or pastry.

Tapas

During the day, most bars and cafés serve small snacks called *tapas*. The word *tapa* means "lid." Some people say that *tapas* were originally small pieces of bread that were placed on top of a drink to keep flies from falling into it. The bar owners then added other foods to the bread to attract more customers. When people began to go to bars especially to eat *tapas*, the bar owners stopped giving them away free. In some places, bar owners still give a few peanuts or a bowl of olives free with a

A variety of tapas *on display in a* tapas *bar. Notice the leg of ham on the back counter.*

drink, but normally you have to pay extra for a *tapa*.

Nowadays people sometimes eat a few different *tapas* instead of having lunch. People usually eat *tapas* at about twelve o'clock so that they do not get too hungry waiting for their late lunch. Having *tapas* is always a good time to meet with friends. Sometimes people gather in big groups and eat their *tapas* standing up. It is considered polite to order extra *tapas* for your friends, even when they say they don't want any.

The typical *tapas* served in most bars are fried prawns, potato omelettes, *ensaladilla rusa* (see the recipe on page 36), and olives. There are other special *tapas* that vary from region to region. Most places near the sea have plenty of fish and shellfish, sardines, anchovies, mussels, and clams for *tapas*. Farther away from the sea, people often eat slices of ham and spicy chorizos.

A busy tapas *bar in Barcelona.*

Fiestas

It is said that you can find a fiesta, or festival, somewhere in Spain every day of the year. Some fiestas can last for days, and they usually include processions, dancing, and singing in the streets. Traditional fiesta foods are *turrón*, a kind of chocolate nougat, and *yemas*, egg yolks boiled in syrup.

Turrón, *a traditional festive food, is made with honey, sugar, chocolate, nuts, and dried fruit.*

Most Spaniards are very religious, and the Roman Catholic religion is an important part of most fiestas. Each town has its own special fiesta in honor of its patron saint, who they believe takes care of the town and its people.

The most important fiesta is *Semana Santa*, the Holy Week leading up to Easter. The *Semana Santa* celebrations in Seville are world famous. Every day and night during the week-long celebrations, statues of the Virgin Mary and Jesus are carried through the streets. Thousands of people wearing special costumes walk in the procession carrying candles while brass bands play.

A Holy Week procession carrying a statue of the Virgin Mary.

According to legend, Santiago (St. James), the patron saint of Spain, is buried at the church of Santiago de Compostela in Galicia. This is the holiest shrine in Spain, visited by pilgrims from all over the world. Every seven years is called the year of St. James. During this special year millions of pilgrims— including the Pope—visit the shrine.

Santiago de Compostela, the shrine of St. James, is visited by thousands of pilgrims every year.

29

A taste of Spain

These giant figures built for Las Fallas *will be set alight on the last night of this three-day fiesta.*

On March 19 there is *Las Fallas* in Valencia. Groups of people spend all year and a great deal of money making huge models of various people or things. Some models can be more than 100 feet high. During *Las Fallas*, the models are put on show in the main squares of the city for three days and nights. On the third night, they are set on fire and there is a fireworks display.

One fiesta in Alicante can get rather messy. At midday, trucks arrive full of tomatoes, and there is an enormous tomato fight that lasts for over an hour. Those who wish to avoid tomato stains stay at home; the rest wear old clothes.

Regional specialties

Cooking traditions and eating habits vary greatly among the seventeen regions of Spain, and there are many regional specialties.

Zarzuela de pescado is a specialty in Catalonia. *Zarzuela* is the Spanish word for a musical or an operetta, and *pescado* is the word for fish. This "musical fish" dish is made by cooking a variety of shellfish in white wine.

Paella is a rice dish made with a variety of different ingredients, depending on what is available. It is cooked in a large two-handled pan, which is also called a paella.

A taste of Spain

Valencia is the home of the famous paella. The basic ingredient is rice, which is cooked with a variety of foods including shellfish, fish, vegetables, and sometimes meat. The word *paella* comes from the Roman word for a pan (the Romans brought rice to Spain). This rice dish is cooked in a special pan, also called a paella, which is large and shallow.

In Aragon, people eat meat cooked in *chilindron* sauce, which is made of sweet red peppers, garlic, and tomatoes.

Red chili peppers drying in the sun. The dried peppers are used for coloring and flavoring chorizos and sauces.

The Basques are famous fishermen, and *Bacalao al pil-pil* is a typical dish from the Basque country. Nowadays *bacalao* is a slang word for house-music, but it really means "cod." *Pil-pil* is a sauce made with chili peppers, garlic, and oil.

Navarre is well known for its river fish, especially trout.

Asturias is home of the *fabada*. This is a delicious stew made with *fabades* (white beans), ham bone, bacon, and *morcilla* (a blood sausage). It is especially good on a cold winter's day.

Galicia is best known for its seafood dishes, which the Galicians like to eat with a local wine called Ribeiro.

Madrid is famed for *cocido*, a type of stew served in two parts: first, the stew is strained and the broth is served by itself; the rest of the stew—a mixture of chickpeas, chicken, and vegetables—is served afterward.

Pisto Manchego, from La Mancha, is a fried vegetable dish that has become a popular dish throughout Spain. La Mancha is also famous for something other than food. Don Quixote and Sancho Panza, two characters from Spain's most famous novel, written by Miguel de Cervantes, came from La Mancha.

In Andalusia, the regional specialty is *huevos a la flamenca*, which means "flamenco eggs." It is a flavorful stew topped with eggs and baked in the oven. *Flamenco* refers to a type of dance that comes from that area. The most famous dish from Andalusia is gazpacho (see the recipe on page 34), a cold soup that is usually served in the summer.

Above *A small farm in Asturias on the north Atlantic coast.*

Above *Miguel de Cervantes and his fictional characters.* Below Huevos a la flamenca.

Gazpacho

Ingredients
Serves 4 to 6

4 large tomatoes
1 green pepper
1 cucumber
2 cloves of garlic
1–2 handfuls of stale
    bread crumbs
5 tablespoons of
    olive oil
white wine vinegar
salt and pepper

Equipment

knife, saucepan
chopping board
garlic crusher
food processor or
    blender
large mixing bowl
slotted spoon

Gazpacho is a famous cold soup from Andalusia in southern Spain.

Before peeling the tomatoes, first place them in a saucepan of boiling water for about half a minute, remove them with a slotted spoon, and pour cold water over them. The skins will come off very easily.

34

1 Peel the tomatoes. Cut off the stalk of the pepper and clean out the seeds. Chop the tomatoes, pepper, and cucumber into small pieces. Crush the garlic.

Always be careful when working with a knife or boiling water. Ask an adult to help.

2 Puree the vegetables and the garlic in a food processor.

4 Pour into a large mixing bowl and stir in about a quart of water, a little bit at a time. Season with salt and pepper and a few dashes of vinegar. Keep tasting the soup while you do this. When you like the consistency and flavor, the soup is ready.

3 Add the bread crumbs and oil to the vegetable mixture. Puree the mixture again.

5 Keep the soup in the refrigerator and serve it cold.

Ensaladilla Rusa

Ingredients

Serves 4 to 6

4 large potatoes
2 medium-sized
  carrots
2 eggs
2 handfuls of pitted
  black olives
3 sweet red peppers
9 oz. tuna fish
1½ cups mayonnaise
water

Equipment

knife
chopping board
2 saucepans
large shallow bowl

*Sweet red peppers
and carrots for sale at
an outdoor market.*

Ensaladilla is a salad that is very
popular as a *tapa* or as a first course.

Always be careful when working with knives. Ask an adult to help you.

3 Chop the olives into small pieces.

1 Peel the potatoes and cut them into small pieces. Wash the carrots and dice them. Put the carrots and potatoes in a saucepan of water, bring to a boil, and simmer for about 15 minutes. Drain the water from the potatoes and carrots and let them cool.

4 Cut the stalks from the peppers and clean out the seeds. Then cut the peppers into small pieces.

5 Put the carrots, potatoes, peppers, olives, tuna fish, chopped egg, and most of the mayonnaise together in a shallow bowl and mix well.

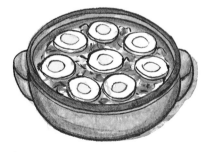

2 While the vegetables are cooking, hard-boil the eggs by putting them in boiling water for about 10 minutes. Let the eggs cool, then peel them. Chop one of the eggs into very small pieces; cut the other into slices.

6 Flatten down the top of the *ensaladilla* and spread the rest of the mayonnaise in a thin layer over the top. Decorate the top with the egg slices. Keep it in the refrigerator until you are ready to serve it.

Pan con tomate y jamón

(Bread with tomatoes and ham)

Ingredients
Serves 4 to 6

1 stick of french bread
(or a loaf of freshly
baked white bread)
2 ripe tomatoes
olive oil
salt
a few slices of ham

Equipment

knife
chopping board

This man is holding a jabuga ham, which is made from pigs that have been fed on acorns. The meat is taken high up into the mountains and cured in the open air.

This snack from Catalonia is quick and easy to prepare.

1   Cut the bread into slices (about half an inch thick).

2   Cut the tomatoes in half.

3   Rub the tomatoes on the slices of bread. Try to leave as much of the flesh of the tomatoes as possible on the bread.

4   Pour a little olive oil onto each slice of bread and season with salt.

5   Put a piece of ham on top of each slice of bread.

Always be careful when working with a knife. Ask an adult to help you.

Horchata

Ingredients
Serves 2

1 cup tigernuts
½ cup sugar
1 qt. water

Equipment
saucepan
food processor
   or blender
bowl
sieve
wooden spoon

Horchata is a very refreshing drink that is served all over Spain. Nowadays it often comes in a bottle, but it is much better when made fresh.

You can buy tigernuts in a health food store. For this recipe, you need to soak the tigernuts in water overnight. Then rinse them well.

1 Heat the water, but do not let it boil.

> Always be careful when heating water. Ask an adult to help you.

2 Put the tigernuts and the hot water into the food processor and puree them until you have a smooth mixture.

3 Press the mixture through the sieve with a wooden spoon.

4 Add the sugar to the mixture and stir it well.

5 Let it cool, and then chill the *horchata* in the refrigerator for about four hours before serving.

Empanada Gallega

(Galician turnover)

A harbor scene in Galicia.

Pan means "bread" in Spanish, and *empanada* means "breaded." *Empanada Gallega* is halfway between a pie and a turnover.

Ingredients

Serves 4

1 medium-sized
    onion
olive oil
flour
8 oz. puff pastry
6½ oz. tuna fish, in
    chunks
paprika and salt
1 egg

Equipment

knife and fork
chopping board
frying pan
wooden spoon
rolling pin
baking tray
bowl
pastry brush
pot holders

1   Peel and chop the onion.

2   Heat a tablespoon of the oil in the frying pan. Fry the onion, stirring it from time to time with a wooden spoon, until it begins to turn golden brown (about 5 minutes). Take it off the heat.

Be careful when heating the oil and chopping the onion. Ask an adult to help you.

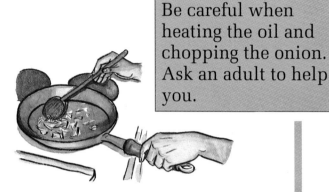

3   Sprinkle a little flour on a clean surface and rub some onto the rolling pin. Roll out the puff pastry. You want to end up with the pastry in two squares, one the same size as the base of the baking tray and the other slightly larger.

A taste of Spain

4   Put a little oil onto the baking tray and rub it around until the bottom is covered.

5   Lay the larger piece of pastry neatly onto the baking tray. Rub a little oil over the top of the pastry.

6   Spread the onion and the chunks of tuna fish on top of the pastry. Season with a little paprika and salt.

7   Crack the egg into a bowl and beat well with a fork.

8   Put the second piece of pastry over the top. Pinch the edges of the two pieces of pastry together so that you have a closed pocket. Make sure you do not leave any gaps in the pastry. Brush the beaten egg over the pastry.

9   Preheat an oven to 400°F. Bake the *empanada* for 25 minutes. Let it cool slightly before serving.

Glossary

Ancestors People from whom we are descended, such as grandparents.

Ancient Belonging to times long past.

Aqueduct A canal that is built to carry water from one area to another.

Archaeologist A person who studies ancient cultures by digging up ancient cities, buildings, or artifacts.

Capital The city that is the seat of the country's government.

Celts An ancient people from central and western Europe.

Citrus fruit A type of acidic fruit covered with thick skin that grows on trees or shrubs in warm climates. Oranges, lemons, limes, and grapefruits are all citrus fruits.

Civil war A war between citizens of the same country.

Conquer To gain control, usually by force, over another group of people.

Cured When referring to food, cured means the food has been smoked or salted to preserve it or to improve the flavor.

Democratic government A system of government in which the people hold the power through elected representatives.

Dialect A variation of a spoken language that is commonly used by a particular group of people.

Dictator A ruler who has complete power and authority over all the people in the country.

Empire A group of countries under the control of another country.

Explorers People who travel to an unknown territory to learn about the land and its people.

Export To sell goods to another country.

Iberian Peninsula The peninsula in southwest Europe occupied by Spain and Portugal.

Irrigation Supplying land with water using a system of channels, ditches, or aqueducts.

Muslims Followers of the religion of Islam and the prophet Mohammed.

Patron saint A saint that is looked upon as a guardian of a person or place.

Peninsula A piece of land that juts out into the sea and is almost completely surrounded by water (from the Latin meaning "almost an island").

Pilgrim A person who makes a trip, or a pilgrimage, to a church, shrine, or other holy place that is important to his or her religion.

Roman Catholic religion A Christian religion. The head of the Roman Catholic Church is the Pope.

Romans People from Rome, Italy. About 2,000 years ago, the ancient Romans ruled over most of Europe and parts of Africa and the Middle East.

Shrine A sacred or holy place.

Stigmas The parts of a flower that receive pollen grains from another plant, which in turn allows a seed to form.

Terrace A flat platform of earth, usually in a series, rising one above the other on the side of a hill.

Traditional A way of doing something that has not changed for years.

Visigoths A branch of the Goths who came from present-day Germany. They invaded the Roman Empire late in the fourth century A.D. and eventually set up a kingdom in Spain.

Picture acknowledgments

The publishers would like to thank the following for allowing their photographs to be reproduced: Anthony Blake Photo Library 21 top, 25, 26, 33 bottom, 34 (all by Gerrit Buntrock); Chapel Studios: Zul *cover inset*, 40; Eye Ubiquitous 16 bottom (Mike Southern); Cephas Picture Library 17, 18 top, 20 bottom (all by Mick Rock), 28 (Roy Stedell); J. Allan Cash 7, 8 top, 10 bottom, 12, 14 both, 15, 16 top, 19 bottom, 38; Greg Evans International Picture Library 10 top, 42 (Benn Keaveney); Explorer 27 bottom (H. Donnezar); Bob Goodwin 21 bottom; Robert Harding Picture Library 9, 23, 30 (Robert Frerck); Anthony King 13, 22, 32, 33 top; Tony Stone Worldwide *cover* (Oliver Benn), *title page* (Tony Caddock), 4 (Robert Frerck), 6 (Tony Craddock), 8 bottom (Manfred Mehlig), 18 bottom (Robert Frerck), 19 top (Alan Smith), 24 (Doug Armand), 29 top (Thomas Ennis), 29 bottom (John Bradley), 36 (Val Corbett); Wayland Picture Library 20 top, 31, 33 middle; Zefa 11.

The map artwork on page 5 was supplied by Peter Bull. The recipe artwork on pages 34 to 44 was supplied by Judy Stevens.

Further information

Information books

Alvarado, Manuel. *Spain.* Countries of the World. New York: Bookwright Press, 1990.

Chrisp, Peter. *Spanish Conquests in the New World.* Exploration and Encounters. New York: Thomson Learning, 1993.

Goldberg, Jake. *Miguel de Cervantes.* Hispanics of Achievement. New York: Chelsea House, 1993.

Selby, Anna. *Spain.* Country Fact Files. Milwaukee: Raintree Steck-Vaughn, 1993.

Wright, Nicola. *Getting to Know: Spain and Spanish.* Getting to Know. Hauppauge, NY: Barron's Educational Series, 1993.

Recipe books

Better Homes and Gardens New Junior Cookbook. Des Moines: Meredith Corp., 1989.

Loewen, Nancy. *Food in Spain.* International Food Library. Vero Beach, FL: Rourke Corp., 1991.

Wilkes, Angela. *My First Cookbook.* New York: Alfred A. Knopf, 1989.

Acknowledgments
The authors wish to thank Michael Jacobs, Elena Horas, and Godfrey and Gillian Goodwin for their assistance and advice.

Index